50 Premium Chicken Dinner Recipes for Home

By: Kelly Johnson

Table of Contents

- Lemon Herb Roasted Chicken
- Chicken Marsala with Wild Mushrooms
- Honey Garlic Glazed Chicken Thighs
- Chicken Piccata with Capers and Lemon
- Balsamic Grilled Chicken with Cherry Tomatoes
- Stuffed Chicken Breast with Spinach and Feta
- Chicken Alfredo with Parmesan Cream Sauce
- Crispy Buttermilk Fried Chicken
- Chicken Cordon Bleu
- Moroccan Spiced Chicken with Couscous
- Garlic Butter Roast Chicken with Thyme
- Chicken Tikka Masala
- Parmesan-Crusted Chicken with Marinara
- Coconut Curry Chicken
- BBQ Chicken with Pineapple Salsa
- Chicken and Mushroom Risotto
- Chicken Kiev
- Jerk Chicken with Mango Chutney
- Slow-Cooked Chicken and Gravy
- Chicken Florentine
- Panko-Crusted Chicken with Lemon Aioli
- Sesame-Ginger Chicken Stir-Fry
- Chicken and Pesto Pasta
- Peruvian Roast Chicken with Aji Verde
- Chicken Scaloppine with Marsala Wine Sauce
- Smoked Paprika Chicken with Roasted Potatoes
- Tuscan Garlic Chicken with Spinach
- Chicken Enchiladas with Green Chile Sauce
- Thai Basil Chicken
- Herb-Crusted Chicken with Dijon Sauce

- Chicken Roulade with Prosciutto and Basil
- Chipotle-Lime Grilled Chicken
- Chicken Parmesan Stuffed Peppers
- Braised Chicken with Olives and Lemon
- Cajun Chicken with Dirty Rice
- Chicken Fricassee with Mushrooms
- Harissa-Spiced Grilled Chicken
- Chicken and Leek Pie
- Honey Mustard Chicken with Sweet Potatoes
- Chicken Saltimbocca
- Chicken and Chorizo Paella
- Butter Chicken with Naan
- Roasted Garlic Chicken with White Wine Sauce
- Chicken Marbella
- Chicken Tagine with Apricots
- Chicken Satay with Peanut Sauce
- Chicken Pot Pie
- Chicken and Asparagus in Cream Sauce
- Crispy Chicken Tenders with Ranch Dip
- Chicken Fajitas with Guacamole

Lemon Herb Roasted Chicken

Ingredients:

- 1 whole chicken (about 4-5 pounds)
- 2 lemons, quartered
- 6 cloves garlic, smashed
- 4 tablespoons olive oil
- 1 tablespoon fresh rosemary, chopped
- 1 tablespoon fresh thyme, chopped
- 1 tablespoon fresh parsley, chopped
- Salt and pepper, to taste
- 1 teaspoon paprika (optional)
- 1 onion, quartered
- 4 sprigs fresh thyme (for garnish)
- 1 cup chicken broth (optional, for basting)

Instructions:

1. Preheat oven to 425°F (220°C).
2. Prepare the chicken: Pat the chicken dry with paper towels. Season the cavity with salt and pepper, then stuff it with lemon quarters, garlic cloves, and onion.
3. Seasoning mix: In a small bowl, combine olive oil, chopped rosemary, thyme, parsley, salt, pepper, and paprika. Rub this mixture all over the outside of the chicken.
4. Tie the legs together with kitchen twine, and tuck the wing tips under the body of the chicken.
5. Roast the chicken: Place the chicken in a roasting pan, breast side up. Roast in the preheated oven for about 1 hour and 15 minutes, or until the internal temperature reaches 165°F (74°C) when checked at the thickest part of the thigh.
6. Baste occasionally with chicken broth or the pan juices to keep the chicken moist.
7. Rest and serve: Remove from the oven, tent with foil, and let it rest for 10-15 minutes before carving. Garnish with fresh thyme and extra lemon slices.

Chicken Marsala with Wild Mushrooms

Ingredients:

- 4 boneless chicken breasts
- Salt and pepper to taste
- 1/2 cup all-purpose flour (for dredging)
- 2 tablespoons olive oil
- 2 tablespoons butter
- 1 cup wild mushrooms, sliced (such as shiitake, cremini, or portobello)
- 3/4 cup Marsala wine
- 1 cup chicken broth
- 1 tablespoon fresh parsley, chopped (for garnish)

Instructions:

1. Season chicken breasts with salt and pepper. Dredge each breast in flour, shaking off excess.
2. In a large skillet, heat olive oil and 1 tablespoon of butter over medium heat. Add chicken breasts and cook for about 5-7 minutes on each side until golden brown and cooked through. Remove chicken from the skillet and set aside.
3. In the same skillet, add the remaining tablespoon of butter and the sliced mushrooms. Sauté until mushrooms are browned and tender, about 5 minutes.
4. Pour in the Marsala wine, scraping the bottom of the skillet to deglaze and release any browned bits. Allow the wine to simmer for about 2-3 minutes.
5. Add the chicken broth and bring to a gentle boil. Cook for an additional 5 minutes to reduce the sauce slightly.
6. Return the chicken to the skillet, spooning the sauce over the top. Cook for another 2-3 minutes to warm through.
7. Serve the chicken garnished with fresh parsley and accompanied by the mushroom sauce. Enjoy!

Honey Garlic Glazed Chicken Thighs
Ingredients:

- 4 bone-in chicken thighs
- 1/4 cup honey
- 3 cloves garlic, minced
- 2 tablespoons soy sauce
- 1 tablespoon apple cider vinegar
- Salt and pepper to taste
- 1 tablespoon olive oil

Instructions:

1. Preheat the oven to 400°F (200°C).
2. In a bowl, whisk together honey, garlic, soy sauce, and apple cider vinegar.
3. Season chicken thighs with salt and pepper. In a large oven-safe skillet, heat olive oil over medium-high heat. Add chicken thighs skin-side down and sear until golden brown, about 5-7 minutes.
4. Flip the chicken and pour the honey garlic mixture over the top.
5. Transfer the skillet to the oven and bake for 25-30 minutes until the chicken is cooked through and the glaze is bubbly.
6. Serve hot, drizzled with the pan sauce.

Chicken Piccata with Capers and Lemon
Ingredients:

- 4 boneless, skinless chicken breasts
- Salt and pepper to taste
- 1/2 cup all-purpose flour (for dredging)
- 4 tablespoons butter
- 2 tablespoons olive oil
- 1/2 cup dry white wine
- 1/4 cup fresh lemon juice
- 2 tablespoons capers
- Fresh parsley, chopped (for garnish)

Instructions:

1. Season chicken breasts with salt and pepper. Dredge each breast in flour, shaking off the excess.
2. In a large skillet, heat 2 tablespoons of butter and olive oil over medium heat. Add the chicken breasts and cook for about 4-5 minutes on each side until golden brown and cooked through. Remove from skillet and set aside.

3. In the same skillet, add white wine and lemon juice, scraping the bottom to deglaze. Stir in capers and simmer for 2-3 minutes.
4. Return the chicken to the skillet, spooning the sauce over the top. Cook for another minute to heat through.
5. Finish with the remaining butter and garnish with fresh parsley before serving.

Balsamic Grilled Chicken with Cherry Tomatoes

Ingredients:
- 4 boneless chicken breasts
- 1/2 cup balsamic vinegar
- 1/4 cup olive oil
- 2 tablespoons honey
- 1 teaspoon garlic powder
- Salt and pepper to taste
- 1 cup cherry tomatoes, halved
- Fresh basil for garnish

Instructions:
1. In a bowl, whisk together balsamic vinegar, olive oil, honey, garlic powder, salt, and pepper.
2. Add chicken breasts to the marinade, ensuring they are well coated. Marinate for at least 30 minutes or up to 2 hours in the refrigerator.
3. Preheat the grill to medium-high heat. Remove chicken from the marinade and grill for 6-7 minutes on each side until cooked through.
4. In the last few minutes of grilling, add cherry tomatoes to the grill, cooking until slightly charred.
5. Serve the chicken topped with grilled cherry tomatoes and garnish with fresh basil.

Chicken Piccata with Capers and Lemon

Ingredients:

- 4 boneless, skinless chicken breasts
- Salt and pepper to taste
- 1/2 cup all-purpose flour (for dredging)
- 4 tablespoons butter
- 2 tablespoons olive oil
- 1/2 cup dry white wine
- 1/4 cup fresh lemon juice
- 2 tablespoons capers
- Fresh parsley, chopped (for garnish)

Instructions:

1. Season chicken breasts with salt and pepper. Dredge each breast in flour, shaking off the excess.
2. In a large skillet, heat 2 tablespoons of butter and olive oil over medium heat. Add the chicken breasts and cook for about 4-5 minutes on each side until golden brown and cooked through. Remove from skillet and set aside.
3. In the same skillet, add white wine and lemon juice, scraping the bottom to deglaze. Stir in capers and simmer for 2-3 minutes.
4. Return the chicken to the skillet, spooning the sauce over the top. Cook for another minute to heat through.
5. Finish with the remaining butter and garnish with fresh parsley before serving.

Balsamic Grilled Chicken with Cherry Tomatoes

Ingredients:

- 4 boneless chicken breasts
- 1/2 cup balsamic vinegar
- 1/4 cup olive oil
- 2 tablespoons honey
- 1 teaspoon garlic powder
- Salt and pepper to taste
- 1 cup cherry tomatoes, halved
- Fresh basil for garnish

Instructions:

1. In a bowl, whisk together balsamic vinegar, olive oil, honey, garlic powder, salt, and pepper.
2. Add chicken breasts to the marinade, ensuring they are well coated. Marinate for at least 30 minutes or up to 2 hours in the refrigerator.
3. Preheat the grill to medium-high heat. Remove chicken from the marinade and grill for 6-7 minutes on each side until cooked through.
4. In the last few minutes of grilling, add cherry tomatoes to the grill, cooking until slightly charred.
5. Serve the chicken topped with grilled cherry tomatoes and garnish with fresh basil.

Stuffed Chicken Breast with Spinach and Feta

Ingredients:

- 4 boneless chicken breasts
- 1 cup fresh spinach, chopped
- 1/2 cup feta cheese, crumbled
- 2 garlic cloves, minced
- 2 tablespoons olive oil
- Salt and pepper, to taste
- Toothpicks or kitchen twine for sealing

Instructions:

1. Preheat oven to 375°F (190°C).
2. Butterfly the chicken breasts by slicing them horizontally without cutting all the way through.
3. In a small bowl, mix the chopped spinach, feta cheese, and garlic.
4. Stuff each chicken breast with the spinach and feta mixture, then secure the edges with toothpicks or kitchen twine.
5. Season the outside of the chicken with salt and pepper.
6. Heat olive oil in an oven-safe skillet over medium-high heat. Sear the chicken breasts on both sides until golden brown.
7. Transfer the skillet to the oven and bake for 20-25 minutes, until the chicken is fully cooked.
8. Remove toothpicks or twine and serve hot.

Chicken Alfredo with Parmesan Cream Sauce

Ingredients:

- 4 boneless chicken breasts
- 2 tablespoons olive oil
- 2 cups heavy cream
- 1 cup grated Parmesan cheese
- 3 garlic cloves, minced
- 1/4 cup unsalted butter
- Salt and pepper, to taste
- Fresh parsley, chopped (for garnish)
- Cooked fettuccine pasta

Instructions:

1. Heat olive oil in a large skillet over medium heat. Season chicken breasts with salt and pepper, then cook for 6-7 minutes on each side until golden and fully cooked. Remove from the skillet and set aside.
2. In the same skillet, melt butter and sauté garlic until fragrant.
3. Add heavy cream and simmer for 3-4 minutes, stirring occasionally.
4. Stir in grated Parmesan cheese until the sauce thickens. Season with salt and pepper to taste.
5. Slice the cooked chicken and add it back to the skillet with the sauce.
6. Serve the chicken and Alfredo sauce over cooked fettuccine pasta. Garnish with chopped parsley and extra Parmesan if desired.

Crispy Buttermilk Fried Chicken

Ingredients:

- 8 chicken drumsticks
- 2 cups buttermilk
- 2 cups all-purpose flour
- 1 teaspoon paprika
- 1 teaspoon garlic powder
- Salt and pepper to taste
- Vegetable oil for frying

Instructions:

1. Marinate the chicken in buttermilk for at least 4 hours or overnight.
2. In a bowl, mix flour, paprika, garlic powder, salt, and pepper.
3. Heat oil in a deep skillet or fryer to 350°F (175°C).
4. Remove chicken from buttermilk, allowing excess to drip off, and coat in the flour mixture.
5. Fry the chicken in batches for about 12-15 minutes until golden brown and cooked through.
6. Drain on paper towels and serve hot.

Chicken Cordon Bleu

Ingredients:

- 4 boneless chicken breasts
- 4 slices of ham
- 4 slices of Swiss cheese
- 1 cup flour
- 2 eggs, beaten
- 2 cups breadcrumbs
- Salt and pepper to taste
- Olive oil for frying

Instructions:

1. Preheat oven to 350°F (175°C).
2. Butterfly the chicken breasts and season with salt and pepper.
3. Place a slice of ham and cheese inside each chicken breast, folding it over to seal.
4. Dredge each chicken breast in flour, dip in beaten eggs, and coat with breadcrumbs.
5. Heat olive oil in a skillet and cook each breast for about 3-4 minutes per side until golden.
6. Transfer to a baking dish and bake for 20-25 minutes until cooked through.
7. Serve with a side of your choice.

Moroccan Spiced Chicken with Couscous

Ingredients:

- 4 chicken thighs
- 2 tablespoons olive oil
- 2 teaspoons cumin
- 1 teaspoon cinnamon
- 1 teaspoon paprika
- Salt and pepper to taste
- 1 cup couscous
- 1 1/4 cups chicken broth
- 1/4 cup raisins
- Fresh cilantro for garnish

Instructions:

1. Preheat oven to 400°F (200°C).
2. Rub the chicken thighs with olive oil, cumin, cinnamon, paprika, salt, and pepper.
3. Place chicken on a baking sheet and roast for 30-35 minutes until cooked through.
4. In a saucepan, bring chicken broth to a boil. Add couscous and raisins, cover, and remove from heat. Let sit for 5 minutes, then fluff with a fork.
5. Serve chicken over couscous and garnish with fresh cilantro.

Garlic Butter Roast Chicken with Thyme

Ingredients:

- 1 whole chicken (about 4-5 pounds)
- 1/2 cup unsalted butter, softened
- 6 garlic cloves, minced
- 2 tablespoons fresh thyme leaves
- Salt and pepper to taste
- 1 lemon, quartered
- Fresh thyme sprigs for garnish

Instructions:

1. Preheat oven to 425°F (220°C).
2. In a bowl, mix softened butter, minced garlic, thyme, salt, and pepper.
3. Pat the chicken dry and loosen the skin over the breasts. Rub half of the garlic butter under the skin and the remaining on the outside.
4. Stuff the cavity with lemon quarters and additional thyme sprigs.
5. Roast the chicken in a baking dish for about 1 hour and 15 minutes or until the internal temperature reaches 165°F (74°C).
6. Let the chicken rest for 10 minutes before carving. Garnish with fresh thyme and serve.

Chicken Tikka Masala

Ingredients:

- 1 pound boneless chicken breast, cut into cubes
- 1 cup plain yogurt
- 2 tablespoons garam masala
- 1 tablespoon turmeric
- 1 tablespoon cumin
- 1 tablespoon coriander
- 1/2 teaspoon chili powder
- 2 tablespoons vegetable oil
- 1 onion, chopped
- 2 garlic cloves, minced
- 1 can (15 oz) tomato sauce
- 1 cup heavy cream
- Fresh cilantro for garnish

Instructions:

1. In a bowl, mix yogurt, garam masala, turmeric, cumin, coriander, and chili powder. Add chicken cubes, cover, and marinate for at least 1 hour or overnight.
2. Heat oil in a large skillet over medium heat. Add onions and sauté until translucent.
3. Add garlic and cook for another minute.
4. Add marinated chicken and cook until browned.
5. Stir in tomato sauce and simmer for 15 minutes.
6. Add heavy cream, stir, and cook for an additional 5 minutes.
7. Garnish with fresh cilantro and serve with rice or naan.

Parmesan-Crusted Chicken with Marinara

Ingredients:

- 4 boneless chicken breasts
- 1 cup breadcrumbs
- 1 cup grated Parmesan cheese
- 1 teaspoon Italian seasoning
- 2 eggs, beaten
- 2 cups marinara sauce
- Olive oil for frying

Instructions:

1. Preheat oven to 375°F (190°C).
2. In a bowl, mix breadcrumbs, Parmesan cheese, and Italian seasoning.
3. Dip each chicken breast in beaten eggs, then coat with the breadcrumb mixture.
4. Heat olive oil in a skillet over medium heat and fry each chicken breast for 3-4 minutes per side until golden.
5. Transfer chicken to a baking dish, cover with marinara sauce, and bake for 20-25 minutes until cooked through.
6. Serve hot, garnished with extra Parmesan if desired.

Coconut Curry Chicken

Ingredients:

- 1 pound boneless chicken thighs, cut into pieces
- 1 can (14 oz) coconut milk
- 2 tablespoons curry powder
- 1 onion, chopped
- 3 garlic cloves, minced
- 1 tablespoon ginger, grated
- 1 bell pepper, sliced
- 2 tablespoons vegetable oil
- Salt to taste
- Fresh cilantro for garnish

Instructions:

1. Heat vegetable oil in a large skillet over medium heat. Add onion, garlic, and ginger, and sauté until fragrant.
2. Add chicken pieces and cook until browned.
3. Stir in curry powder and cook for another minute.
4. Pour in coconut milk and bring to a simmer.
5. Add sliced bell pepper and season with salt.
6. Simmer for 15-20 minutes until the chicken is cooked through and the sauce thickens.
7. Garnish with fresh cilantro and serve with rice or naan.

BBQ Chicken with Pineapple Salsa

Ingredients:

- 4 boneless chicken breasts
- 1 cup BBQ sauce
- 1 cup fresh pineapple, diced
- 1/4 cup red onion, finely chopped
- 1/4 cup cilantro, chopped
- Juice of 1 lime
- Salt and pepper to taste

Instructions:

1. Preheat grill to medium-high heat.
2. Season chicken breasts with salt and pepper and brush with BBQ sauce.
3. Grill chicken for 6-7 minutes on each side until fully cooked.
4. In a bowl, combine diced pineapple, red onion, cilantro, lime juice, salt, and pepper to make the salsa.
5. Serve grilled chicken topped with pineapple salsa.

Chicken and Mushroom Risotto

Ingredients:

- 1 cup Arborio rice
- 4 cups chicken broth
- 1 cup mushrooms, sliced
- 1 onion, chopped
- 2 garlic cloves, minced
- 1/2 cup white wine (optional)
- 1/2 cup Parmesan cheese, grated
- 2 tablespoons olive oil
- Salt and pepper to taste
- Fresh parsley for garnish

Instructions:

1. In a saucepan, heat chicken broth and keep warm.
2. In a large skillet, heat olive oil over medium heat. Sauté onion and garlic until translucent.
3. Add sliced mushrooms and cook until tender.
4. Stir in Arborio rice and cook for 1-2 minutes.
5. Pour in white wine (if using) and stir until absorbed.
6. Gradually add warm chicken broth, one ladle at a time, stirring constantly until absorbed before adding more. Continue until rice is creamy and al dente (about 18-20 minutes).
7. Stir in Parmesan cheese, salt, and pepper. Garnish with fresh parsley before serving.

Chicken Kiev

Ingredients:

- 4 boneless chicken breasts
- 1/2 cup unsalted butter, softened
- 2 garlic cloves, minced
- 2 tablespoons fresh parsley, chopped
- 1 teaspoon lemon juice
- 1 cup flour
- 2 eggs, beaten
- 2 cups breadcrumbs
- Salt and pepper to taste
- Oil for frying

Instructions:

1. Preheat oven to 350°F (175°C).
2. In a bowl, mix softened butter, garlic, parsley, lemon juice, salt, and pepper.
3. Butterfly the chicken breasts, place a tablespoon of the butter mixture inside, and seal them.
4. Dredge each chicken breast in flour, dip in beaten eggs, and coat with breadcrumbs.
5. Heat oil in a skillet and fry each chicken breast until golden brown on both sides.
6. Transfer to a baking sheet and bake for 20-25 minutes until cooked through.

Jerk Chicken with Mango Chutney

Ingredients:

- 4 chicken thighs
- 2 tablespoons jerk seasoning
- 1 tablespoon olive oil
- 1 cup mango, diced
- 1/4 cup red onion, chopped
- 1/4 cup cilantro, chopped
- Juice of 1 lime
- Salt and pepper to taste

Instructions:

1. Preheat grill to medium-high heat.
2. Rub chicken thighs with jerk seasoning and olive oil.
3. Grill chicken for 6-8 minutes on each side until cooked through.
4. In a bowl, mix diced mango, red onion, cilantro, lime juice, salt, and pepper to make the chutney.
5. Serve grilled chicken topped with mango chutney.

Slow-Cooked Chicken and Gravy

Ingredients:

- 4 boneless chicken breasts
- 1 can (10.5 oz) cream of chicken soup
- 1 cup chicken broth
- 1 onion, chopped
- 2 garlic cloves, minced
- 1 teaspoon dried thyme
- Salt and pepper to taste

Instructions:

1. Place chicken breasts in the slow cooker.
2. In a bowl, mix cream of chicken soup, chicken broth, onion, garlic, thyme, salt, and pepper.
3. Pour the mixture over the chicken breasts.
4. Cover and cook on low for 6-8 hours or high for 3-4 hours until chicken is tender.
5. Serve hot with rice or mashed potatoes, drizzling gravy over the top.

Chicken Florentine

Ingredients:

- 4 boneless chicken breasts
- 4 cups fresh spinach
- 1 cup heavy cream
- 1/2 cup grated Parmesan cheese
- 2 garlic cloves, minced
- 2 tablespoons olive oil
- Salt and pepper to taste

Instructions:

1. In a large skillet, heat olive oil over medium heat. Season chicken breasts with salt and pepper, then cook for 6-7 minutes per side until golden brown and cooked through. Remove from the skillet and set aside.
2. In the same skillet, add minced garlic and sauté for about 1 minute.
3. Add fresh spinach and cook until wilted.
4. Pour in heavy cream and stir in Parmesan cheese, simmering until the sauce thickens.
5. Return chicken to the skillet, coating it with the creamy spinach sauce. Serve hot.

Panko-Crusted Chicken with Lemon Aioli

Ingredients:

- 4 boneless chicken breasts
- 1 cup panko breadcrumbs
- 1/2 cup all-purpose flour
- 2 eggs, beaten
- Salt and pepper to taste
- 1/4 cup mayonnaise
- 1 tablespoon lemon juice
- 1 teaspoon garlic powder
- Olive oil for frying

Instructions:

1. Preheat oven to 375°F (190°C).
2. Set up a breading station with flour, beaten eggs, and panko breadcrumbs mixed with salt and pepper.
3. Dredge each chicken breast in flour, dip in eggs, then coat in panko breadcrumbs.
4. Heat olive oil in a skillet over medium heat and fry each chicken breast for 3-4 minutes on each side until golden.
5. Transfer to a baking dish and bake for an additional 10-15 minutes until cooked through.
6. For the aioli, mix mayonnaise, lemon juice, garlic powder, salt, and pepper. Serve chicken with lemon aioli on the side.

Sesame-Ginger Chicken Stir-Fry

Ingredients:

- 1 pound boneless chicken breast, sliced
- 2 cups mixed vegetables (bell peppers, broccoli, carrots)
- 3 tablespoons soy sauce
- 1 tablespoon sesame oil
- 1 tablespoon ginger, grated
- 2 garlic cloves, minced
- 2 tablespoons sesame seeds
- Cooked rice for serving

Instructions:

1. In a large skillet or wok, heat sesame oil over medium-high heat.
2. Add sliced chicken and cook until browned and cooked through.
3. Stir in garlic and ginger, cooking for another minute.
4. Add mixed vegetables and soy sauce, stir-frying until vegetables are tender-crisp.
5. Sprinkle sesame seeds over the stir-fry before serving. Serve hot over cooked rice.

Chicken and Pesto Pasta

Ingredients:

- 4 boneless chicken breasts
- 8 ounces pasta of choice
- 1 cup basil pesto
- 1/2 cup cherry tomatoes, halved
- 1/4 cup grated Parmesan cheese
- Salt and pepper to taste
- Olive oil for cooking

Instructions:

1. Cook pasta according to package instructions; drain and set aside.
2. In a skillet, heat olive oil over medium heat. Season chicken breasts with salt and pepper, then cook for 6-7 minutes per side until cooked through. Slice the chicken.
3. In a large bowl, combine cooked pasta, pesto, cherry tomatoes, and sliced chicken. Toss to combine.
4. Serve hot, garnished with Parmesan cheese.

Peruvian Roast Chicken with Aji Verde

Ingredients:

- 1 whole chicken (about 4-5 pounds)
- 3 tablespoons olive oil
- 2 tablespoons paprika
- 1 tablespoon cumin
- 1 tablespoon garlic powder
- Salt and pepper to taste
- 1 cup cilantro, chopped
- 1 jalapeño, seeded
- 1/4 cup mayonnaise
- Juice of 1 lime

Instructions:

1. Preheat oven to 425°F (220°C).
2. In a bowl, mix olive oil, paprika, cumin, garlic powder, salt, and pepper to create a marinade. Rub this mixture all over the chicken.
3. Roast the chicken in a baking dish for about 1 hour and 15 minutes or until the internal temperature reaches 165°F (74°C).
4. For the aji verde, blend cilantro, jalapeño, mayonnaise, lime juice, salt, and pepper until smooth.
5. Serve the roasted chicken with aji verde on the side.

Chicken Scaloppine with Marsala Wine Sauce

Ingredients:

- 4 boneless chicken breasts, pounded thin
- 1/2 cup all-purpose flour
- 1/4 cup olive oil
- 1 cup mushrooms, sliced
- 1 cup Marsala wine
- 1/2 cup chicken broth
- Salt and pepper to taste
- Fresh parsley for garnish

Instructions:

1. Dredge the chicken breasts in flour, shaking off excess.
2. In a large skillet, heat olive oil over medium heat. Add the chicken and cook until golden brown on both sides, about 3-4 minutes per side. Remove from the skillet and set aside.
3. In the same skillet, add sliced mushrooms and sauté until tender.
4. Pour in the Marsala wine and chicken broth, scraping the bottom of the skillet to deglaze.
5. Return chicken to the skillet and simmer for an additional 5-7 minutes until the sauce thickens.
6. Garnish with fresh parsley before serving.

Smoked Paprika Chicken with Roasted Potatoes

Ingredients:

- 4 boneless chicken thighs
- 2 tablespoons smoked paprika
- 2 tablespoons olive oil
- 1 teaspoon garlic powder
- Salt and pepper to taste
- 4 cups baby potatoes, halved
- Fresh parsley for garnish

Instructions:

1. Preheat oven to 400°F (200°C).
2. In a bowl, mix smoked paprika, olive oil, garlic powder, salt, and pepper. Rub this mixture onto the chicken thighs.
3. Place halved potatoes on a baking sheet and drizzle with olive oil, salt, and pepper. Toss to coat.
4. Nestle the seasoned chicken thighs among the potatoes.
5. Roast for 25-30 minutes or until the chicken is cooked through and potatoes are tender.
6. Garnish with fresh parsley before serving.

Tuscan Garlic Chicken with Spinach

Ingredients:

- 4 boneless chicken breasts
- 2 tablespoons olive oil
- 4 garlic cloves, minced
- 2 cups fresh spinach
- 1 cup heavy cream
- 1/2 cup sun-dried tomatoes, chopped
- 1/2 cup grated Parmesan cheese
- Salt and pepper to taste

Instructions:

1. In a large skillet, heat olive oil over medium heat. Season chicken breasts with salt and pepper, then cook until golden brown and cooked through. Remove from skillet and set aside.
2. In the same skillet, add minced garlic and sauté for about 1 minute.
3. Add fresh spinach and sun-dried tomatoes, cooking until spinach is wilted.
4. Pour in heavy cream and stir in Parmesan cheese, simmering until thickened.
5. Return chicken to the skillet, coating it in the sauce. Serve hot.

Chicken Enchiladas with Green Chile Sauce

Ingredients:

- 4 cups shredded cooked chicken
- 8 flour tortillas
- 2 cups green chile enchilada sauce
- 1 cup shredded cheese (cheddar or Monterey Jack)
- 1/2 cup sour cream
- 1/4 cup chopped cilantro

Instructions:

1. Preheat oven to 350°F (175°C).
2. In a bowl, mix shredded chicken with 1/2 cup of enchilada sauce and 1/4 cup of cheese.
3. Spoon the chicken mixture into each tortilla, roll them up, and place in a greased baking dish seam-side down.
4. Pour remaining enchilada sauce over the rolled tortillas and top with remaining cheese.
5. Bake for 20-25 minutes until cheese is bubbly and golden.
6. Serve hot with sour cream and garnish with cilantro.

Thai Basil Chicken

Ingredients:

- 1 pound boneless chicken breast, sliced
- 2 tablespoons vegetable oil
- 3 garlic cloves, minced
- 1 red bell pepper, sliced
- 1/4 cup soy sauce
- 1 tablespoon oyster sauce
- 1 tablespoon sugar
- 1 cup fresh basil leaves

Instructions:

1. In a large skillet or wok, heat vegetable oil over medium-high heat.
2. Add minced garlic and sauté for about 30 seconds.
3. Add sliced chicken and cook until browned.
4. Stir in red bell pepper, soy sauce, oyster sauce, and sugar.
5. Cook for an additional 3-4 minutes until the chicken is cooked through.
6. Remove from heat and stir in fresh basil leaves until wilted. Serve hot over rice.

Herb-Crusted Chicken with Dijon Sauce

Ingredients:

- 4 boneless chicken breasts
- 1 cup breadcrumbs
- 1/2 cup grated Parmesan cheese
- 2 tablespoons fresh herbs (thyme, rosemary, or parsley)
- 1/4 cup Dijon mustard
- Olive oil for drizzling

Instructions:

1. Preheat oven to 375°F (190°C).
2. In a bowl, mix breadcrumbs, Parmesan cheese, and fresh herbs.
3. Brush each chicken breast with Dijon mustard, then coat with the breadcrumb mixture.
4. Place on a baking sheet and drizzle with olive oil.
5. Bake for 25-30 minutes until the chicken is cooked through and the crust is golden.

Chicken Roulade with Prosciutto and Basil

Ingredients:

- 4 boneless chicken breasts
- 4 slices prosciutto
- 1/2 cup fresh basil leaves
- 1/2 cup mozzarella cheese, shredded
- Salt and pepper to taste
- Olive oil for cooking

Instructions:

1. Preheat oven to 375°F (190°C).
2. Place chicken breasts between plastic wrap and pound them to an even thickness. Season with salt and pepper.
3. Lay slices of prosciutto, basil leaves, and mozzarella cheese on each chicken breast.
4. Roll up the chicken tightly and secure with toothpicks.
5. Heat olive oil in a skillet and sear the chicken roulades until golden brown on all sides.
6. Transfer to a baking dish and bake for 20-25 minutes until cooked through. Remove toothpicks before serving.

Chipotle-Lime Grilled Chicken

Ingredients:

- 4 boneless chicken breasts
- 2 tablespoons chipotle powder
- 1/4 cup lime juice
- 2 tablespoons olive oil
- 2 garlic cloves, minced
- Salt and pepper to taste

Instructions:

1. In a bowl, mix chipotle powder, lime juice, olive oil, garlic, salt, and pepper to create a marinade.
2. Add chicken breasts to the marinade, cover, and refrigerate for at least 30 minutes.
3. Preheat grill to medium-high heat.
4. Grill chicken for 6-7 minutes on each side until cooked through.
5. Serve hot, garnished with lime wedges if desired.

Chicken Parmesan Stuffed Peppers

Ingredients:

- 4 bell peppers, halved and seeds removed
- 2 cups cooked shredded chicken
- 1 cup marinara sauce
- 1 cup shredded mozzarella cheese
- 1/2 cup grated Parmesan cheese
- 1 teaspoon Italian seasoning
- Salt and pepper to taste

Instructions:

1. Preheat the oven to 375°F (190°C).
2. In a bowl, combine shredded chicken, marinara sauce, Italian seasoning, salt, and pepper.
3. Stuff each bell pepper half with the chicken mixture and place in a baking dish.
4. Top with shredded mozzarella and grated Parmesan cheese.
5. Cover with foil and bake for 25-30 minutes.
6. Remove foil and bake for an additional 10 minutes, until the cheese is bubbly and golden. Serve hot.

Braised Chicken with Olives and Lemon

Ingredients:

- 4 bone-in chicken thighs
- 1 cup green olives, pitted
- 1 lemon, sliced
- 1 onion, sliced
- 3 garlic cloves, minced
- 1 cup chicken broth
- 2 tablespoons olive oil
- Salt and pepper to taste

Instructions:

1. In a large pot, heat olive oil over medium-high heat. Season chicken thighs with salt and pepper, then brown on both sides.
2. Remove chicken and set aside. In the same pot, add onion and garlic, cooking until softened.
3. Return chicken to the pot and add chicken broth, olives, and lemon slices.
4. Cover and simmer for 30-40 minutes until the chicken is cooked through.
5. Serve hot with pan juices.

Cajun Chicken with Dirty Rice

Ingredients:

- 4 boneless chicken breasts
- 2 tablespoons Cajun seasoning
- 1 cup cooked rice
- 1/2 cup bell pepper, chopped
- 1/2 cup onion, chopped
- 1/2 cup celery, chopped
- 1 cup chicken broth
- 2 tablespoons olive oil

Instructions:

1. Season chicken breasts with Cajun seasoning.
2. In a skillet, heat olive oil over medium heat. Cook chicken until browned and cooked through, about 6-7 minutes per side. Remove and set aside.
3. In the same skillet, add bell pepper, onion, and celery. Sauté until softened.
4. Stir in cooked rice and chicken broth, cooking until heated through.
5. Slice chicken and serve over the dirty rice.

Chicken Fricassee with Mushrooms

Ingredients:

- 4 boneless chicken thighs
- 2 cups mushrooms, sliced
- 1 onion, chopped
- 2 cups chicken broth
- 1 cup heavy cream
- 2 tablespoons olive oil
- Salt and pepper to taste
- Fresh parsley for garnish

Instructions:

1. In a large skillet, heat olive oil over medium heat. Season chicken thighs with salt and pepper and brown on both sides. Remove and set aside.
2. In the same skillet, add onions and mushrooms, cooking until softened.
3. Return chicken to the skillet and pour in chicken broth. Simmer for 20 minutes.
4. Stir in heavy cream and cook for an additional 10 minutes until thickened.
5. Garnish with fresh parsley before serving.

Harissa-Spiced Grilled Chicken

Ingredients:

- 4 boneless chicken breasts
- 3 tablespoons harissa paste
- 2 tablespoons olive oil
- 1 lemon, juiced
- Salt and pepper to taste

Instructions:

1. In a bowl, mix harissa paste, olive oil, lemon juice, salt, and pepper.
2. Add chicken breasts and marinate for at least 30 minutes.
3. Preheat grill to medium-high heat.
4. Grill chicken for 6-7 minutes on each side until cooked through.
5. Serve hot with your favorite side dishes.

Chicken and Leek Pie

Ingredients:

- 2 cups cooked shredded chicken
- 2 leeks, sliced
- 1 cup chicken broth
- 1 cup heavy cream
- 1 sheet puff pastry
- 1 tablespoon olive oil
- Salt and pepper to taste

Instructions:

1. Preheat the oven to 400°F (200°C).
2. In a skillet, heat olive oil over medium heat. Add leeks and sauté until softened.
3. Stir in chicken broth and heavy cream, cooking until thickened.
4. Add shredded chicken, salt, and pepper, mixing well.
5. Transfer the mixture to a baking dish and cover with puff pastry, sealing the edges.
6. Bake for 25-30 minutes until the pastry is golden brown. Serve hot.

Honey Mustard Chicken with Sweet Potatoes

Ingredients:

- 4 boneless chicken breasts
- 1/4 cup honey
- 1/4 cup Dijon mustard
- 2 sweet potatoes, cubed
- 2 tablespoons olive oil
- Salt and pepper to taste

Instructions:

1. Preheat the oven to 400°F (200°C).
2. In a bowl, mix honey, Dijon mustard, salt, and pepper. Coat chicken breasts in the mixture.
3. On a baking sheet, toss cubed sweet potatoes with olive oil, salt, and pepper.
4. Place chicken on the same baking sheet.
5. Bake for 25-30 minutes until chicken is cooked through and sweet potatoes are tender. Serve hot.

Chicken Saltimbocca

Ingredients:

- 4 boneless chicken breasts
- 8 slices prosciutto
- 12 fresh sage leaves
- 1/2 cup all-purpose flour
- 1/4 cup olive oil
- 1/2 cup white wine
- Salt and pepper to taste

Instructions:

1. Preheat the oven to 350°F (175°C).
2. Lay two slices of prosciutto on each chicken breast and top with sage leaves.
3. Dredge the chicken in flour, shaking off excess.
4. In a large skillet, heat olive oil over medium heat. Cook the chicken for 3-4 minutes on each side until golden brown.
5. Pour in white wine and simmer for 5 minutes until the sauce reduces.
6. Transfer the chicken to the oven and bake for 10 minutes. Serve with the pan sauce.

Chicken and Chorizo Paella

Ingredients:

- 1 pound boneless chicken thighs, chopped
- 1 cup chorizo, sliced
- 2 cups arborio rice
- 1 onion, chopped
- 2 cloves garlic, minced
- 1 red bell pepper, chopped
- 1 teaspoon smoked paprika
- 4 cups chicken broth
- 1 cup peas
- Olive oil for cooking
- Salt and pepper to taste

Instructions:

1. In a large skillet, heat olive oil over medium heat. Add chicken and chorizo, cooking until browned. Remove and set aside.
2. In the same skillet, add onion, garlic, and red bell pepper, sautéing until softened.
3. Stir in arborio rice and smoked paprika, cooking for 1-2 minutes.
4. Pour in chicken broth and bring to a boil. Reduce heat, cover, and simmer for 15 minutes.
5. Add the chicken, chorizo, and peas, cooking for an additional 5-10 minutes until rice is tender. Serve hot.

Butter Chicken with Naan

Ingredients:

- 1 pound boneless chicken thighs, cubed
- 1/2 cup plain yogurt
- 2 tablespoons butter
- 1 onion, chopped
- 2 cloves garlic, minced
- 1 tablespoon ginger, grated
- 1 can (14 oz) crushed tomatoes
- 1 tablespoon garam masala
- 1 cup heavy cream
- Salt to taste
- Naan bread for serving

Instructions:

1. Marinate the chicken in yogurt for at least 30 minutes.
2. In a large skillet, melt butter over medium heat. Add onion, garlic, and ginger, sautéing until softened.
3. Add the marinated chicken and cook until browned.
4. Stir in crushed tomatoes and garam masala, simmering for 10 minutes.
5. Stir in heavy cream and cook for an additional 5 minutes. Serve hot with naan bread.

Roasted Garlic Chicken with White Wine Sauce

Ingredients:

- 4 bone-in chicken thighs
- 1 head garlic, roasted
- 1/2 cup white wine
- 1 cup chicken broth
- 2 tablespoons olive oil
- Salt and pepper to taste
- Fresh parsley for garnish

Instructions:

1. Preheat the oven to 375°F (190°C).
2. Season chicken thighs with salt and pepper. In a large oven-safe skillet, heat olive oil over medium-high heat. Brown the chicken on both sides.
3. Squeeze roasted garlic cloves into the skillet. Pour in white wine and chicken broth.
4. Transfer the skillet to the oven and roast for 25-30 minutes until chicken is cooked through.
5. Garnish with fresh parsley before serving.

Chicken Marbella

Ingredients:

- 4 bone-in chicken thighs
- 1/2 cup green olives, pitted
- 1/2 cup prunes, pitted
- 1/4 cup capers
- 1/2 cup white wine
- 1/4 cup olive oil
- 1/4 cup red wine vinegar
- 1 tablespoon brown sugar
- Fresh parsley for garnish

Instructions:

1. Preheat the oven to 350°F (175°C).
2. In a large baking dish, combine olives, prunes, capers, white wine, olive oil, red wine vinegar, and brown sugar.
3. Nestle the chicken thighs into the mixture, coating them well.
4. Bake for 45 minutes to 1 hour until chicken is cooked through.
5. Garnish with fresh parsley before serving.

Chicken Tagine with Apricots

Ingredients:

- 4 boneless chicken thighs
- 1 onion, chopped
- 2 cloves garlic, minced
- 1 teaspoon ground cumin
- 1 teaspoon ground cinnamon
- 1 cup chicken broth
- 1 cup dried apricots, halved
- 2 tablespoons olive oil
- Salt and pepper to taste
- Fresh cilantro for garnish

Instructions:

1. In a large pot or tagine, heat olive oil over medium heat. Add onion and garlic, sautéing until softened.
2. Season chicken thighs with salt, pepper, cumin, and cinnamon. Add to the pot and brown on all sides.
3. Pour in chicken broth and add dried apricots. Cover and simmer for 30-40 minutes until chicken is tender.
4. Garnish with fresh cilantro before serving.

Chicken Satay with Peanut Sauce

Ingredients:

- 1 pound boneless chicken breasts, cut into strips
- 1/4 cup soy sauce
- 2 tablespoons brown sugar
- 2 tablespoons lime juice
- 1 tablespoon ground coriander
- 1 tablespoon ground cumin
- Skewers for grilling

Peanut Sauce:

- 1/2 cup peanut butter
- 2 tablespoons soy sauce
- 1 tablespoon honey
- 1 tablespoon lime juice
- 1/2 cup coconut milk

Instructions:

1. In a bowl, mix soy sauce, brown sugar, lime juice, coriander, and cumin. Add chicken strips and marinate for at least 30 minutes.
2. Preheat the grill to medium-high heat. Thread chicken onto skewers.
3. Grill chicken for about 5-7 minutes on each side until cooked through.
4. For the peanut sauce, whisk together peanut butter, soy sauce, honey, lime juice, and coconut milk until smooth.
5. Serve chicken satay with peanut sauce for dipping.

Chicken Pot Pie

Ingredients:

- 2 cups cooked shredded chicken
- 1 cup carrots, diced
- 1 cup peas
- 1/2 cup celery, diced
- 1/2 cup onion, chopped
- 1/3 cup butter
- 1/3 cup flour
- 1 3/4 cups chicken broth
- 1/2 cup milk
- 1 teaspoon thyme
- Salt and pepper to taste
- 1 pie crust

Instructions:

1. Preheat the oven to 425°F (220°C).
2. In a skillet, melt butter over medium heat. Add onions, carrots, celery, and cook until softened.
3. Stir in flour, cooking for 1 minute, then gradually add chicken broth and milk. Cook until thickened.
4. Add chicken, peas, thyme, salt, and pepper.
5. Pour filling into a pie crust, top with another crust, and seal edges. Cut slits in the top crust for steam to escape.
6. Bake for 30-35 minutes until golden brown. Let cool slightly before serving.

Chicken and Asparagus in Cream Sauce

Ingredients:

- 1 pound boneless chicken breasts, sliced
- 1 bunch asparagus, trimmed and cut into pieces
- 1 cup heavy cream
- 2 tablespoons olive oil
- 2 cloves garlic, minced
- 1/2 cup grated Parmesan cheese
- Salt and pepper to taste

Instructions:

1. In a skillet, heat olive oil over medium heat. Add sliced chicken and cook until browned and cooked through. Remove and set aside.
2. In the same skillet, add garlic and asparagus, cooking until asparagus is tender.
3. Stir in heavy cream and Parmesan cheese, cooking until the sauce thickens.
4. Return chicken to the skillet, mixing well. Season with salt and pepper. Serve hot.

Crispy Chicken Tenders with Ranch Dip

Ingredients:

- 1 pound chicken breasts, cut into strips
- 1 cup breadcrumbs
- 1/2 cup flour
- 2 eggs, beaten
- 1 teaspoon garlic powder
- Salt and pepper to taste
- Oil for frying

Ranch Dip:

- 1/2 cup sour cream
- 1/2 cup mayonnaise
- 1 tablespoon ranch seasoning mix

Instructions:

1. In three separate bowls, place flour, beaten eggs, and breadcrumbs mixed with garlic powder, salt, and pepper.
2. Dredge chicken strips in flour, dip in egg, and coat with breadcrumbs.
3. In a skillet, heat oil over medium-high heat. Fry chicken tenders until golden brown and cooked through.
4. For the ranch dip, mix sour cream, mayonnaise, and ranch seasoning until well combined.
5. Serve chicken tenders with ranch dip.

Chicken Fajitas with Guacamole

Ingredients:

- 1 pound boneless chicken breasts, sliced
- 1 bell pepper, sliced
- 1 onion, sliced
- 2 tablespoons olive oil
- 2 teaspoons fajita seasoning
- Salt and pepper to taste
- Flour tortillas for serving

Guacamole:

- 2 ripe avocados
- 1 lime, juiced
- 1/2 onion, chopped
- 1 tomato, diced
- Salt to taste

Instructions:

1. In a skillet, heat olive oil over medium heat. Add chicken and cook until browned.
2. Add bell pepper, onion, fajita seasoning, salt, and pepper, cooking until vegetables are tender.
3. For the guacamole, mash avocados in a bowl and mix in lime juice, onion, tomato, and salt.
4. Serve chicken fajitas in warm tortillas with guacamole on the side.

www.ingramcontent.com/pod-product-compliance
Lightning Source LLC
LaVergne TN
LVHW081327060526
838201LV00055B/2504